Michelle Kwan

QUEST FOR GOLD

BY
MARK STEWART
AND
MIKE KENNEDY

THE MILLBROOK PRESS
BROOKFIELD, CONNECTICUT

M

THE MILLBROOK PRESS

Produced by
BITTERSWEET PUBLISHING, John Sammis, President
and
TEAM STEWART, INC.

Series Design and Electronic Page Makeup by
JAFFE ENTERPRISE, Ron Jaffe

All photos courtesy AP/ Wide World Photos, Inc. except the following:
SportsChrome — Cover, Pages 53, 54
AllSport — Pages 7 (Doug Pensinger), 15 (Chris Cole), 16 (Jed Jacobsohn),
17 (Mike Powell), 19, 23 (Brian Bahr), 27 top (Phil Cole), 42 (Doug Pensinger),
44 (Mike Powell), 46 (Jamie Squire), 48 (Jamie Squire)
The following images are from the collection of Team Stewart:
Lambert & Butler © 1914 — Page 9
Sports Illustrated for Kids © 2000 — Page 10
Sports Illustrated for Kids © 1996 — Page 27 (bottom)
Sports Illustrated © 1968 — Page 30
Sports Illustrated © 1998 — Page 43
Sports Illustrated for Women © 2001 — Page 63
People Magazine © 1994 — Page 22
TV Guide © 1998 — Page 38

Published by
The Millbrook Press, Inc.
2 Old New Milford Road
Brookfield, Connecticut 06804

www.millbrookpress.com

Library of Congress Cataloging-in-Publication Data

Stewart, Mark.
   Michelle Kwan : quest for gold / by Mark Stewart and Mike Kennedy.
      p. cm.
   Includes index.
   Summary: Reviews the career and life of Chinese-American figure skater
Michelle Kwan, who has won five U.S. Nationals and an unprecedented four
World Championships, as she looks forward to the 2002 Olympics.
   ISBN 0-7613-2622-7 (lib. bdg.)
      1. Kwan, Michelle, 1980—Juvenile literature. 2. Skaters—United States—
Bibliography—Juvenile literature. 3. Women skaters—United States—
Biography—Juvenile literature. [1. Kwan, Michelle, 1980- 2. Ice skaters. 3.
Chinese Americans—Biography. 4. Women—Biography.] I. Kennedy, Mike
(Mike William), 1965- II. Title.

GV850.K93 S84 2002
796.91'2'092—dc21
[B]   2001045012

1 3 5 7 9 10 8 6 4 2

Contents

California Girls

CHAPTER 1

"We had no vacations. No days off. We skated on Christmas Day."
KAREN KWAN

If you were a sports champion, what would make you keep competing once you had won everything in sight? Would it be the roar of the crowd? The publicity? The trophies and awards? What would make you prove yourself every day when you had nothing left to prove? For Michelle Kwan, winning is still the ultimate goal. But the reason she has stayed atop her sport for so long is because she *loves* it. Nothing can compare to the rush she feels every time she glides across the ice, whether she is on an empty practice rink or in front of 20,000 people.

"Ever since I started skating, I've always dreamed what it would be like to be a skater, an ice princess," Michelle says. "I've always dreamed that my life would be as it is now. So there's nothing I would change. This is what I wished for."

Few athletes can honestly say they are living out their dreams.
Michelle Kwan is one of the lucky few who can.

Torrance is known more for its beaches and its industry than for its figure skating fame.

Michelle grew up in one of the last places you would expect to find a figure skating champion: Southern California. She was born on July 7, 1980, in the city of Torrance, which is best known for its surfing, in-line skating, and swimming. Michelle's father, Danny, came to California with his family in the early 1970s from Canton, China. He worked for the telephone company. Michelle's mother, Estella, came to California with her family from Hong Kong at about the same time. They met and married, then

Did You Know?

Michelle's grandmother gave her a gold dragon necklace when she was a child. She never takes it off.

started a business together, the Golden Pheasant restaurant. Danny and Estella also

Did You Know?

Michelle's given name is Kwan Wing Shan. Her friends call her "Shelley"

started a family. Their first child, Ron, was born in 1976. Two years later Karen came along. Michelle was the Kwans' third and final child.

Ron was a very good athlete. His favorite sport was hockey, which was just beginning to get popular in Southern California. He joined a team in Torrance when he was nine. Karen and Michelle would sometimes go to the rink to watch him practice. One day, the girls asked if they could skate, too. "My first skating memory is from when I was six," recalls Michelle. "I was wearing rental skates and eating Nerds candy."

Karen and Michelle were naturals. Each had unusually good balance, and neither was afraid to fall. Before long, the girls wanted to learn how to perform the tricks they saw figure skaters do on television. Their parents agreed to hire a coach if they promised to stick with it. Lessons were very expensive. To save money, Estella worked extra hours at the Golden Pheasant, and Danny chipped in after he came home from work. "Skating cost a lot of money, and it was a burden for everyone in the family," Michelle's father remembers. "We were taking the kids skating from five to eight A.M., and then I'd go to work, and they'd go to school. I told them, 'I don't mind doing it, but you have to make a commitment.'"

Brian Boitano takes to the air during the 1988 Olympics. He won gold at the U.S. Nationals, World Championships, and Olympics that year, inspiring Michelle to become a great skater.

Less than a year after her first lesson, Michelle won the first competition she ever entered. Excited about her progress and convinced she would become a star, she began to dream about her future. Michelle saw every second of the figure skating competition at the 1988 Winter Olympics, and watched in awe as U.S. skater Brian Boitano won a gold medal. This was now her goal.

Over the next two years, Michelle devoted all her free time to training. She loved skating so much she practiced even when she was sick with the flu and chicken pox. Although Karen stayed with her younger sister stride for stride, it was becoming clear that there was something special about Michelle. When others watched them skate, their eyes were immediately drawn to Michelle. Some sisters would have become jealous, but not the Kwans. They thought of themselves as a team. They helped and supported and pushed each other. And when they could skate no more, their parents were there to keep them focused. "One day, I'd be tired, the next day Michelle would be tired," Karen remembers. "But Dad would tell us, 'It's your responsibility to do it even when you don't want to.'"

Something Old, Something New

The moves you see Michelle Kwan and other top figure skaters perform are a mix of old and new. The basics (like the toe spin) have been around for more than a century; some of the jumping combinations you will see at upcoming competitions have only been perfected in the last few months!

Since the very first organized figure skating events, competitors have been required to execute certain moves, and they have been judged on how well they accomplish this task. When you watch a skater's "short program" today, you are seeing the modern version of this very old tradition.

LAMBERT & BUTLER'S CIGARETTES.

A TOE SPIN.

The "long program" is a skater's chance to really show off her athletic and artistic talents. In the early years of the 20th century, skaters wore long dresses and jumping was actually illegal. In fact, there was not much artistry in the sport at all.

This changed with the arrival of an 11-year-old Norwegian girl named Sonja Henie. She believed that figure skating should be more like ballet. At the 1924 Olympics, Henie dazzled the crowd with her jumps and spins, and her youthful energy. By the 1928 Olympics, the rules had been amended to allow this type of skating, and the sport took off.

The one thing that has never changed in figure skating is the important role that judging plays. Although judges are supposed to be looking for the same qualities in all skaters, they are human beings—they make mistakes, they play favorites, and they can be influenced by things they are supposed to ignore, such as a skater's costume, hair, and makeup, or the music she selects.

Back in the old days days, there were two primary complaints about judging. Judges were suspected of being too generous when it came to awarding points to skaters from their own country, and they differed too much in their views of what was "artistic" and what wasn't.

Well, guess what? Today the same accusations are being made!

The truth is that the "people factor" will never leave skating. And that is a good thing. If you were to take the emotion out of the sport—if the human element were removed—no one would watch it anymore. The drama and beauty would disappear, and wonderful athletes like Michelle Kwan would look for challenges in other sports.

Ice Princess

CHAPTER 2

"I love to put myself
through the competition
and stress and pressure."
MICHELLE KWAN

BY 1990, the Kwans were beginning to realize that their daughters might be elite-level skaters. There was only one way to find out, and that was to let them compete against the best. This would require more advanced training than they could get where they lived. They had heard of a man named Frank Carroll, who worked with skaters at the prestigious Ice Castle International Training Center a few hours north, in Lake Arrowhead, California. Carroll had also heard of Karen and Michelle—or "Big Kwan" and "Little

MICHELLE KWAN

Sports Illustrated KiDS

Age 11

FIGURE SKATER ◆ LAKE ARROWHEAD, CALIFORNIA

Collectors love this *SI FOR KIDS* card, which depicts Michelle at age 11.

Frank Carroll, flanked by the Kwan sisters. After just a few workouts,
he realized both girls could be world-class skaters.

Kwan," as they had come to be known in skating circles. The Kwans agreed to pay
Carroll to drive to Torrance and train their daughters once a week.

In less than a year, Carroll was convinced the Kwan sisters were prodigies. They
required full-time training, he told Estella and Danny. Carroll said he could arrange for
dual scholarships from the Ice Castle International Skating Foundation, so that the girls
could move to Lake Arrowhead at little or no expense to the Kwans. But they were worried that their daughters were too young to live so far from home. Of course, Karen
and Michelle were dying to go—and eventually they convinced their parents to let
them move away.

Michelle adored the training facilities at the Ice Castle. The practice rink is considered one of the finest in the world.

During the girls' first year at the Ice Castle, their father drove to Lake Arrowhead almost every day to spend time with them. Estella usually stayed at the house in Torrance to look after Ron, who was now in high school. Karen and Michelle, meanwhile, were having the time of their lives. They were smart and outgoing, so getting straight A's and making friends were easy. And because they had each other, they were never homesick, like so many of the other young skaters. When they got bored, the girls

Did You Know?

Frank Carroll's reputation for molding children into champions was a big reason the Kwans let their kids move north to the Ice Castle. Linda Fratianne (above), Tiffany Chin, and Christopher Bowman had come to Carroll as promising youngsters, and each had gone on to accomplish great things.

would pop over to a nearby mall, or go sledding in the San Gabriel mountains, which surrounded the skating complex. The rink itself was magnificent—it made their three hours of daily skating practice just fly by.

The intensive training began paying dividends almost immediately. A few months after she arrived at the Ice Castle, Karen qualified for the 1991 U.S. Figure Skating Championships in Minneapolis, Minnesota. Though Michelle was not eligible to compete, she joined her father and sister on the trip anyway. In hindsight, she wished she had remained in Lake Arrowhead. In order for Michelle to practice, she had to use a tiny outdoor rink. As she skated in the cold and thought about the others working out

> "It wasn't until I got to the Ice Castle...that I realized what a rookie I was."
>
> *MICHELLE KWAN*

inside, she vowed never to attend another event unless she was going to compete.

After Karen and Michelle had been at the Ice Castle a year or so, the Kwan family decided some changes had to be made. Danny was worn to a frazzle from all the driving, and Estella missed her daughters badly. Estella rented a tiny cabin in Lake Arrowhead and Karen and Michelle moved in with her. It was a tight squeeze for three people, and it got even tighter whenever Ron and his dad came for a visit. "Everything was jammed in," Michelle laughs. "My sister, my mom, dad, and brother once in a while. We were all living in that one room with a toilet. It was the size of a bedroom."

During this time, Michelle's talent blossomed. She improved dramatically in all areas, but particularly in her jumps. Michelle had just the right combination going for her—her legs were powerful, her body graceful, and her timing impeccable. Sometimes it looked as if she were bouncing on a trampoline, not whooshing across the ice.

Michelle shares a laugh with her grandfather, Ho Yuen Kwan, during a family celebration at the Golden Pheasant.

Coach Carroll pleaded with Michelle to be patient and work her way up to ladies' competition. She did not listen.

Michelle entered the Junior Nationals early in 1992 and finished ninth. Although she could hold her own with any girl in the country, there were still some rough edges to her routine. Michelle needed more experience. This frustrated her. She knew she had the skills to skate in ladies' competitions, and it was annoying to think how long it would take before she qualified for these events. Coach Carroll pleaded with Michelle to trust him and be patient, and repeatedly denied her requests to be tested for this level of competition. He felt that the pressure of competing at this level would impede her progress.

One weekend when Carroll was out of town, Michelle saw her chance. She told her father that she had already mastered the skills to be a world-class skater, and that passing the test would be a breeze. She failed to mention that her coach had asked her to wait. Danny Kwan gave his permission and, as Michelle expected, she easily passed the test. She would now be allowed to enter her sport's most challenging competitions.

Carroll was furious when he returned. He informed Michelle that her little prank had just cost her *all* of her free time. Now she would have to train twice as hard, just to keep from looking like an idiot. The 11-year-old replied that she was ready. "I didn't want to finish my homework and watch four hours of TV," Michelle remembers. "I wanted to get to the 1994 Olympics."

At the age of 11, Michelle felt she was ready to move up to the top level of figure skating.

Jumping for Joy

CHAPTER 3

"At my first Nationals,
people said, 'She's
the jumping bean.'"

MICHELLE KWAN

Frank Carroll was accustomed to bringing his skaters along at a pace that he alone chose. Suddenly he had a near-impossible task on his hands. Michelle had not won a major competition as a junior; now she had to go up against the world's top women. Some would be twice her age! Carroll's first move was to bring in a choreographer named Lori Nichol. Nichol's job was to design routines that would show off Michelle's more developed skills, while de-emphasizing the things she still needed to work on.

Michelle, meanwhile, began training like an Olympian. She spent extra hours at the rink, and hit the weight room to build up her tiny body. Leaps she had been fooling around with just a few months earlier had suddenly become serious. As a junior, executing a perfect triple jump or a double axel was a cause for celebration. Now she would be *expected* to nail them *every* time. When she wasn't on the ice or pumping iron, Michelle was working with a ballet teacher to develop more grace. And then, when all

12-year-old Michelle glides to a sixth-place finish at the 1993 U.S. nationals.

of her skating stuff was done, she still had her schoolwork to do! Carroll arranged for a private tutor so Michelle could make the most of every minute.

People around the Ice Castle began to worry about Michelle. They had never seen someone so young become so completely consumed by the sport. She no longer went to class, and had little time to do anything other than eat and sleep when she was not working on her skating. They were concerned that Michelle would be expecting too much of herself, and would be crushed when she saw just how tough her opponents were. The plan was to enter six events in 1993 to give the 12-year-old a "taste" of competition.

As it turned out, Michelle's friends and family had nothing to fear. It was the *competition* that got crushed, as Michelle went out and won four of the six events she entered. At the U.S. Olympic Festival, she took the ice before the largest crowd in the

Tonya Harding (left) and Nancy Kerrigan pose together at the Olympics trials in Detroit.

history of figure skating and calmly landed six triple jumps. The audience was on its feet when she finished, and tears of joy rolled down the cheeks of everyone who knew her. It had been 20 years since a girl so young skated at the Olympic Festival—and Michelle placed first!

What once had been a little girl's silly dream no longer seemed so far-fetched. Michelle's incredible 1993 season put her in consideration for one of the three spots on the U.S. Olympic team that would go to Lillehammer, Norway, in February 1994. The two best skaters would compete for the gold medal, while the third would travel as an "alternate" in case one suffered an injury. As the Olympic trials approached, most of the attention was focused on the three favorites for the team: Nancy Kerrigan, Tonya Harding, and Nicole Bobek. They were mature, veteran skaters who were right up there with the best in the world.

Michelle is in control during the 1994 Olympic trials. She finished second to Tonya Harding.

The sport of figure skating had become incredibly popular during the 1980s and early 1990s. The skaters who did well at the 1994 Olympics stood to make millions of dollars skating in ice shows, doing commercials, and endorsing products. The pressure to make the team was incredible, and this led to one of the most bizarre incidents in sports history. Harding's husband, Jeff Gillooley, paid a man to assault Kerrigan. As she was coming off the ice after a practice session, the hired assailant smashed her knee with a heavy metal baton. Luckily, the injury was not permanent. But Kerrigan was unable to skate in the trials. The whole world was now watching to see what would happen next. Michelle, who was practically forgotten in the madness, performed extremely well and finished ahead of everyone except Harding, whom police had not yet connected to the assault. Against all odds, Michelle had made the Olympic team!

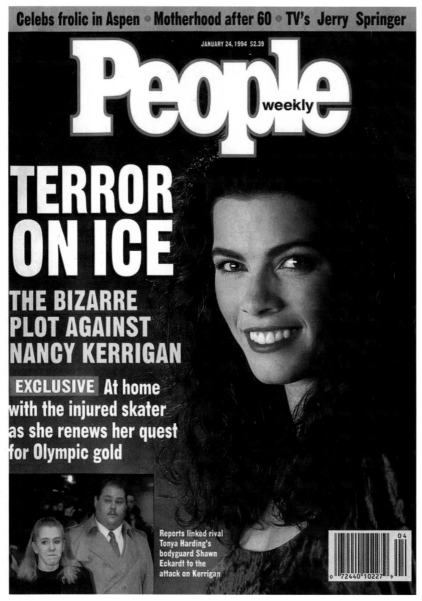

Celebs frolic in Aspen • Motherhood after 60 • TV's Jerry Springer

JANUARY 24, 1994 $2.39

People weekly

TERROR ON ICE

THE BIZARRE PLOT AGAINST NANCY KERRIGAN

EXCLUSIVE At home with the injured skater as she renews her quest for Olympic gold

Reports linked rival Tonya Harding's bodyguard Shawn Eckardt to the attack on Kerrigan

0 72440 10227 9

The bizarre plot against Nancy Kerrigan was front-page news in January of 1994.

Or had she? In the days that followed, evidence surfaced that suggested Harding had known about the attack but had done nothing to stop it. At first, U.S. Figure Skating officials wanted to throw Harding off the team, but they did not have enough proof against her. They had to let her skate. The next dilemma they faced was what to do with Kerrigan. She made a rapid recovery from her injuries, and it seemed very unfair to deny her a spot while Harding was allowed to skate. The decision was made to give Michelle's spot to Kerrigan, bumping Michelle back to the alternate role.

Like everyone across the country, Michelle had been following the story with great interest. She admired Kerrigan and thought it was unfortunate for her to lose her shot

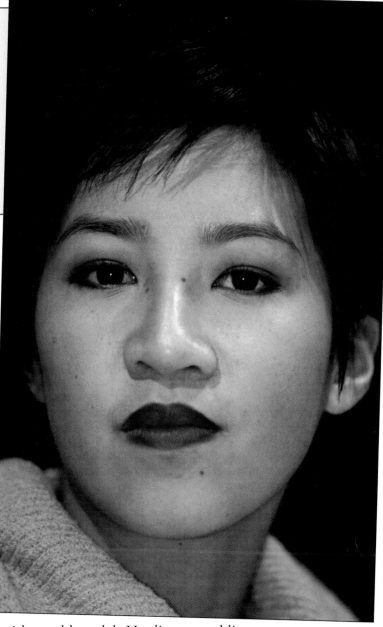

> "It didn't feel like an Olympic experience. I never really got to see the ice rink. I never got to see the Olympic Village."
>
> *MICHELLE KWAN*

at Olympic gold because of a freak injury. Still, Michelle was devastated by the news that she probably would not compete. The best she could do was to put on a smile and say the right thing. "I think it's fair," she told reporters. "What I've gotten already is incredible."

Michelle went to the Olympics, but she felt like an outsider. She watched on television with the rest of the world as Kerrigan was edged by Oksana Baiul, a 15-year-old Ukrainian orphan whose incredible story ended with a gold medal. Harding, crumbling under the weight of her guilt, skated poorly and did not win a medal. Michelle felt bad for Nancy. It seemed that it was her destiny to win after all she had been through. As Michelle would learn for herself, destiny can be a tricky thing.

Figuring It All Out

CHAPTER 4

*"When she's skating,
she looks like
someone much older"*
FRANK CARROLL

Michelle spent the rest of 1994 trying to establish herself on the figure skating circuit. She made her first appearance in the World Championships and finished a disappointing eighth, but placed no lower than third in the rest of the events she entered that season. At the U.S. Ladies' Outdoor Challenge, Michelle skated to a first-place finish.

The next year brought several changes to Michelle's life. With her brother away at college and her father retired from the phone company, the family could finally live together in one place. They found a roomy house in Lake Arrowhead and settled in. Michelle was now used to the endless hours of practice, and was staying on top of her schoolwork, but the details of her schedule often made her head spin. Hotel and airline reservations, practices, public appearances—life on the road was a little too much for

Mistakes like this, at the Goodwill Games, showed that Michelle had room for improvement. Still, the 1994 season was a fantastic one.

Michelle and Karen at practice for the 1995 U.S. Nationals. It was the first time in 36 years that sisters had competed together in this event.

her to comprehend. To ease the burden, Michelle's parents hired a man named Shep Goldberg to be her manager.

With her routine set and a support team in place, Michelle set out to conquer her sport in 1995. She entered nine events and finished first in five. For most skaters, this would be a spectacular year. But Michelle felt like a failure after making critical errors

"It's always hard when people are criticizing you. You're trying your best. It's not like I sit home watching TV all the time."

MICHELLE KWAN

in the two most important events. At the U.S. Nationals, she messed up a double-jump combination in the short program and dropped to third. To make matters worse, she was the last skater in the long program. It was a position that made her nervous. Michelle hated to wait around and watch everyone else before she took her turn. This time she fell midway through her routine while attempting a triple-lutz—a jump that might have helped her get back into first place. At the World Championships, in England, Michelle unveiled a new short pro-gram, but the judges hated it and gave her low marks. The next day, after her long program, she got poor scores again. Michelle thought she had done well both times. What was going on?

Coach Carroll explained. Michelle was no longer the sprightly little "jumping bean"—she had grown seven inches and gained more than 20 pounds since her first ladies' competition. She was now one of the most powerful and athletic skaters in the world. But judges, Carroll said, look for more than technical merit in a skater's performance. They award points for the emotion and elegance her routine conveys. In

Michelle's first trading card is highly prized among figure skating fans.

"A talent like Michelle's is easy to take for granted. She's so graceful that she doesn't appear to have to work at it. But it takes a lot of work."

PAUL WYLIE

Michelle's case, she was lagging behind the competition in this area. The good news was that, as all young skaters do, Michelle was already developing a "signature" style. The trick was to mold this into something so beautiful that it would sweep judges and spectators off their feet. Carroll and Nichol felt that people were already passionate about Michelle's athleticism; now they had to create a new look that also would bring out her natural beauty.

The first thing to go was the little-girl wardrobe. Michelle was a lovely young woman and judges had to start seeing her this way. Her hair and makeup also needed to reflect this change. Next, Michelle needed a brand-new "grown-up" routine for her long program. Carroll and Nichol put their heads together and came up with the story of Salome, a sultry, provocative character from the Bible.

Danny and Estella Kwan were not happy about Michelle's new look,
but they were overjoyed at the success she achieved in 1996.

Michelle was crazy about the new "her." Danny and Estella Kwan were not as
enthusiastic. A traditional theme in Chinese culture forbids girls to dress and act as
adult women, and Michelle's sexy costume and daring routine went way over the line.
Almost all Asian parents face this dilemma when their teenagers become Americanized;
it can be a difficult time. For the Kwans, it was made easier by the fact that they already
had decided to back their daughters' skating careers. Like it or not, there was no turning back now.

U.S. OLYMPIC CHAMPION PEGGY FLEMING

America fell in love with teenager Peggy Fleming in the 1960s. Like Michelle, she appeared on lots of magazine covers.

The impact of the changes in Michelle's on-ice image were astounding. At the 1996 U.S. Nationals the 15-year-old became the youngest champion since Peggy Fleming won in 1964. From there, Michelle won almost every event she entered. Her list of titles included the ISU Championship Series Final, Continent's Cup, Skate America, Trophee Lalique, and Cotton Incorporated Ultimate Four. At the World Championships, Michelle was at her very best. Going into her long program, she trailed only China's Lu Chen, who had skated the two best routines of her life. Michelle knew she had to give a magical performance, and she delivered. With more pressure and drama than she had ever experienced in her life, she dazzled the crowd and earned two perfect scores from the judges. For months Michelle had felt that she was the best skater in the world. Now she had the gold medal to prove it.

Michelle and Coach Carroll react to the two perfect 6's she received from judges at the 1996 World Figure Skating Championships.

The Year That Wasn't

CHAPTER 5

> "I want to be a legend,
> like Dorothy Hamill
> and Peggy Fleming."
> MICHELLE KWAN

As the 1997 season began, Michelle was poised to take her place among history's elite skaters. She had a string of nine championships in a row, her autobiography *Heart of a Champion* was about to be published, and she was already being compared to Dorothy Hamill, whose combination of style, charm, and athleticism inspired an entire generation of skaters in the early 1980s. This kind of praise fueled Michelle's competitive fire. She was ready to conquer the world.

Then a weird thing happened. Michelle went into a long slump. Just as hitters lose their batting eye or basketball players lose their shooting touch, Michelle kept making tiny mistakes without knowing why. In most sports, you can survive a minor error. In figure skating, you cannot. In one event after another, Michelle goofed up just enough to keep her from winning.

Michelle was flattered by comparisons to Dorothy Hamill, pictured here at the 1975 World Championships. Her signature move was called the "Hamill Camel."

Nicole Bobek, one of the emerging U.S. stars who pushed Michelle to keep improving

Her "coma," as she calls it today, started in February at the 1997 U.S. Nationals in Nashville, Tennessee. No one was given a chance of unseating Michelle as American champion, and it showed in the routines of the other skaters. Most seemed to be skating for second place. But a precocious 14-year-old named Tara Lipinski ignored the hype and went right after Michelle. Lipinski was not part of the figure skating mainstream—her parents did not have a lot of money, and at times she had to practice at rinks in shopping malls. Skating with a hunger, she applied tremendous pressure on Michelle, who had to pull out all the stops in her long program in order to defend her title. Midway through the routine, Michelle attempted a difficult triple-toe/triple-toe combination and fell on the second jump. Unnerved, she fell again moments later. "I was standing up, then I was on the ice, and it was like, 'What happened?'" Michelle recalls. "I panicked."

In the months that followed, Michelle could not shake that feeling of uncertainty. After finishing second at the ISU Champions Series Final—an event she had won eas-

Scott Hamilton, whose illness deeply affected Michelle in 1997.

ily the year before—she no longer appeared confident on the ice. There were a lot of theories on Michelle's decline, but none of them seemed to provide any answers. Perhaps the best belonged to Michelle's father. He sensed that she had forgotten what she loved about figure skating in the first place. Michelle's focus on winning, he believed, was keeping her from enjoying herself on the ice.

There were other things weighing on Michelle's mind. One of her favorite skaters, Scott Hamilton, announced that he had cancer. Then, right before the World Championships in Switzerland, Carlo Fassi died of a heart attack. Fassi was Nicole Bobek's coach, but he was a friend to all the skaters.

Michelle was feeling especially low after skating a so-so short program at the Worlds. At the end of the first day she was in fourth place. In the locker room that evening, everything came crashing in. Michelle was getting ready to go back to the hotel when she popped a shoelace. Her eyes welled up with tears and a few seconds later she began sobbing.

Carol Heiss-Jenkins dominated her sport from 1957 to 1960. She believes Michelle could stay on top even longer.

After a good cry, Michelle started seeing things more clearly. She still loved skating, but this was no longer evident in her routines. Somewhere along the way she had lost her enthusiasm, and the judges had definitely noticed. Michelle had two days before she had to skate her long program, two days to pull herself together and recapture the special feeling she had the year before. She decided the best way to get past the sadness was to think about everything she loved about skating. When the time came to take the ice again, Michelle was simply radiant. She brought down the house with her long program, moving with breathtaking elegance to a selection from William Alwyn's *Lyra Angelica*. "When I hear that music, it always reminds me of angels and clouds," Michelle says. "That's what I was thinking of while skating. That I'm free, and I'm going to cloud nine."

Though she finished second overall, Michelle felt reborn. More important, her fresh attitude caught the attention of people throughout the sport. "Michelle's capable of doing these types of performances more than once," noted Carol Heiss-

Did You Know?

In 1996, Karen Kwan decided to put aside skating and concentrate on her education. She enrolled in Boston College with an eye on becoming a journalist. From time to time, Karen would give pointers to skaters in the Boston area, but did not tell anyone she was related to Michelle. "Only my close friends know about my connection to Michelle," she smiles.

Jenkins, a former Olympic champion who became a top coach. "She's so mentally strong, she could do it all over again in Nagano."

Nagano, Japan, the site of the 1998 Olympics, was still a year away. During that time Michelle had to keep up her momentum and re-establish herself as the world's top skater. She made enormous strides with victories at Skate America and Skate Canada toward the end of 1997, but then a setback came. That fall, she began feeling intense pain in her left foot. X-rays revealed a stress fracture in her second toe. Michelle was fitted with a special cast and told by her doc-

After coming out of her 1997 "coma," Michelle set her sights on winning Olympic gold in 1998.

A confident and mature Michelle graces the cover of *TV GUIDE'S* Olympic Preview.

tors to stay off the ice for a month.

Michelle could not remember a time in her life when she had gone so long without skating. Although her body stayed in good condition through exercise, her mind began to play tricks on her. She began to realize that the 1998 Olympics might be her last, and started to wonder what would happen if she failed to win the gold medal. There are four years between Olympic Games and a lot can happen during that time. Michelle looked at the top skaters from 1994. Most had turned professional and joined touring ice shows. None was considered a threat at the 1998 Games.

Where would Michelle be in 2002? Who could say? The more she thought about it, the more pressure she felt to win at Nagano.

The Kwan File

Michelle's Favorite . . .

COLOR
   Turquoise

FOODS
   Lasagna & Sushi

DESSERT
   Cookies 'n Cream Ice Cream

ACTRESS
   Julia Roberts

ACTOR
   Leonardo DiCaprio

CHARITY
   Children's Miracle Network

ATHLETE
   Michael Jordan

MALE SKATERS
   Brian Boitano & Elvis Stojko

MUSICIANS
   Tori Amos, Jewel, &
   Natalie Merchant

Did You Know?

Michelle offers the same advice to her fans,
whether they are interested in skating or not:
"Work hard, be yourself, and have fun!"

No Pain, No Gain

CHAPTER 6

"This is amazing!
I made the Olympic team.
It's like, 'Wow.'"
MICHELLE KWAN

Michelle's cast came off and she was cleared to skate again around Christmas. She had been warned that she would not be pain-free, but did not realize what this meant until she began to practice. The pain in her foot was still excruciating at times, hardly better than before. Michelle even thought about skipping the U.S. Nationals in January. Although the top finishers at this event typically make the Olympic team, the federation can hold a spot open for an injured skater (as it had in the case of Nancy Kerrigan). Was Michelle's reputation strong enough to merit this kind of consideration? After some careful thinking, she concluded it was not. Michelle decided not to risk missing the Olympics. She would endure the pain, and try to win a spot.

Michelle quickly worked her way back into top form. She learned how to skate through the discomfort without losing her composure. With a week to go before the Nationals, she was back to her pre-injury practice regimen. The night of the short pro-

Michelle shows reporters the good luck dragon necklace her grandmother gave her as a child. She would need more than luck to win the gold medal in Nagano.

gram, all eyes were on Michelle. She performed the required moves flawlessly, and did so with a maturity and elegance that bowled over the judges. Skating to Rachmaninoff's *Finale*, she earned seven perfect scores!

> "It wasn't so much what she did, as the way she did it. She had a look of ease in her face, an aura. It was one of her best moments."
>
> *FRANK CARROLL, ON MICHELLE'S SHORT PROGRAM AT THE 1998 NATIONALS*

With the audience and judges now in the palm of her hand, Michelle wrapped up the national title and a spot on the Olympic team with a memorable performance in the long program. She got perfect scores from eight judges, one of whom summed up her routine by saying, "She floated. She enjoyed every second. She savored it."

Now it was time to get down to business. Michelle returned to Lake Arrowhead to train for the Olympics and continue treatment on her stress fracture, which still had not healed completely. She found that rest made her foot feel better, but of course she had to practice, too. Achieving the correct balance between the two, she believed, might prove the difference between a good performance in Japan and a great one.

Michelle leaps across the cover of *SPORTS ILLUSTRATED'S* 1998 Olympic Guide. Many in the media thought she was a "sure thing" to win the gold medal.

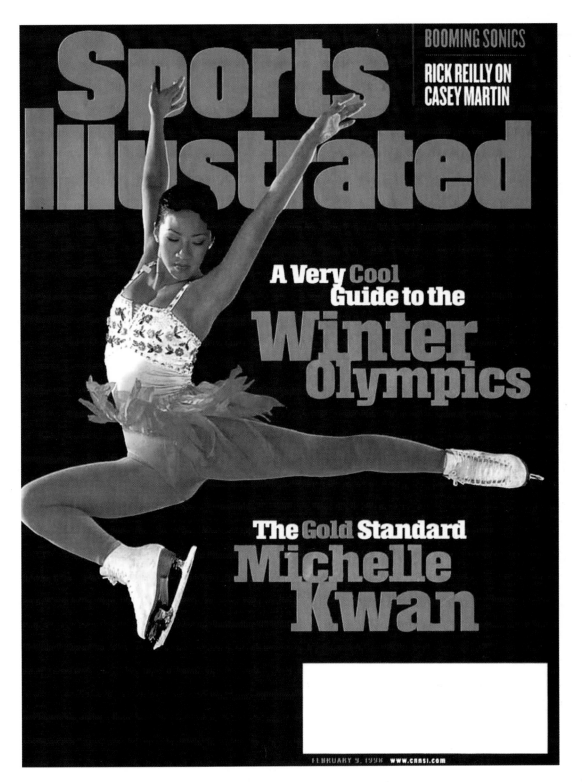

Sports Illustrated

BOOMING SONICS

RICK REILLY ON CASEY MARTIN

A Very Cool Guide to the Winter Olympics

The Gold Standard Michelle Kwan

FEBRUARY 9, 1998 WWW.CNNSI.COM

Tara Lipinski, Michelle's main competition at the 1998 Olympics

That is why Michelle chose to fly to Nagano several days early. Getting used to the new environment and the time change was just the start, however. Michelle and her parents also rented a large hotel suite instead of staying in the Olympic Village with the other athletes. She wanted no distractions.

Michelle's chief competition for the gold medal would be Tara Lipinski. While Michelle shut herself away and stuck mostly to the practice rink and hotel, Lipinski soaked up every last drop of the Olympic Village experience. Rather than distracting her, the nonstop fun seemed to relax the bubbly Lipinski. And she skated freely and flawlessly during the short program. Michelle skated brilliantly, too—in fact, she was

Michelle finishes her long program at the 1998 Olympics.
She skated well, but her performance seemed to be missing something.

As her scores are posted, Michelle realizes that she has given Tara Lipinski a chance to beat her.

the leader after the first day. However, those familiar with Michelle could not help noticing that she seemed a little tentative. Coach Carroll, for one, told Michelle that she seemed too worried about making a mistake. Skate with the same energy, strength, and freedom you did at the Nationals, he said, and you're all but guaranteed to win the gold.

Unfortunately, Michelle did not take his advice. In the long program, she skated cleanly but without much emotion. Although she did not make any noticeable errors, again she seemed a bit hesitant at times. Michelle's scores, though very good, left a slight opening for Lipinski. The plucky 15-year-old sensed the opportunity and glided, twirled, and soared as if she hadn't a care in the world. When she finished, the crowd roared with wild enthusiasm. When her scores were posted Lipinski shrieked with delight. She had snatched the gold from Michelle by the slimmest of margins. Suddenly, Michelle knew exactly how Nancy Kerrigan must have felt four years earlier.

Michelle was badly shaken. In the days that followed, she replayed everything leading up to the Olympics in her mind, searching for something to explain how her dreams had been so suddenly and unexpectedly dashed. Should she have lived in the Olympic Village? Did she arrive in Japan too early? Too late? Did she worry too much about being perfect? Or not enough? Maybe she had been kidding herself. Maybe she never *was* the best skater in the world.

Michelle was so confused that she even considered retiring. To her, a silver medal seemed worthless, which meant *she* was worthless. "Everything happened so fast, I didn't appreciate what I'd already done," she says. "I didn't enjoy it. I was so worried about winning, it was as if I was caught up in my own web. I kept asking myself, 'Why am I here if I don't love it? Why am I torturing myself?' It's supposed to be fun, and I thought I'd die if I didn't win."

Gold medalist Tara Lipinski (center), silver medalist Michelle Kwan, and bronze medalist Lu Chen (right) wave to the crowd.

Bounce Back

CHAPTER 7

"The Salt Lake City Games
are going to be amazing.
I'll be back."
MICHELLE KWAN

Michelle Kwan is a smart young women. It did not take long for her to see things for what they were. She had lost. She had not *died*. And although Michelle had not fully achieved her dream, she had accomplished something very special. "I had three wishes," she says. "One was to make the Olympics. The second was to skate well there. The third was to win the gold medal. Two wishes came true."

Determined to reclaim her crown, Michelle destroyed the competition at the 1998 World Championships and went on a memorable roll. She placed first in five of the next six events. More important, she learned from past mistakes and began to search for greater harmony in her personal life. At one point during the year, Michelle took a whole month off from skating. And after acing her final exams and graduating from high school with a B+ average, she rewarded herself by dressing up and attending the

After brooding over her second-place finish in Japan,
Michelle pulled herself together and began making positive changes in her life.

Meeting actor
Leonardo DiCaprio in
1998 was a huge thrill for Michelle.

premiere of the movie *Titanic*. She even got to meet her all-time favorite actor, Leonardo DiCaprio. So complete was Michelle's "recovery" from the disappointment in Nagano that she was named 1998 Sportswoman of the Year by the Women's Sports Foundation.

Michelle soon set her sights on the 2002 Olympics, in Salt Lake City, Utah. As great as it would have been to win gold in Japan, the thought of winning it on U.S. soil, in front of her "home" fans, was even more appealing to her. That meant making a three-year plan that would have Michelle in peak form for the Games. She and Coach Carroll agreed that they would have to increase the difficulty of her routines. Thanks to Oksana Baiul, Tara Lipinski, and Michelle, figure skating had become a sport dominated by young girls. Smaller, lighter skaters can do things in the air that more mature skaters cannot, and the judges seemed to be rewarding the younger competitors and penalizing the older ones. Most observers believed this trend would start to reverse itself by 2002, but that the judges would still be expecting something spectacular from potential gold medalists. So Michelle started adding treacherous triple-jump combinations to her long program.

Michelle's three-year plan also included quality time *off* the ice. She did not want to burn out, and she did not want to miss the fun her friends were having at college. Michelle and Karen—now a student at Boston University—spoke all the time, and it sure sounded like Karen was enjoying campus life. Michelle applied to Harvard,

Stanford, and UCLA, and was accepted at all three. She eventually chose UCLA, because it was close to home and close to the Ice Castle.

The first step toward Salt Lake City was the 1999 U.S. Nationals. Michelle unveiled her new triple-jumps and wowed the judges. Right on her tail, however, was Naomi Nari Nam, a 13-year-old Californian who stood just four feet tall. Had Michelle skated her Nagano routine again, she might have lost. As it was, she barely edged the spectacular Nam for her third U.S. title—the difference was a stunning triple-toe/triple-toe combination in the long program. Michelle finished the 1999 season with a silver medal at the World Championships and victories at the Keri Lotion Figure Skating Classic, Masters of Figure Skating, and Skate America.

That September, she began classes at UCLA. Juggling the academic and social demands of college with a strict skating regimen was not easy. Add to that a television deal with Disney, an endorsement contract with Chevrolet, and her own video game, and Michelle had more than enough to keep her busy. That became clear a couple of months later, when she finished behind Russia's Irina Slutskaya at Skate Canada. Michelle had needed to turn it up a notch and rework her routines before the event, but she could not because she was studying for exams. She made the choice to do well in school, and was willing to live with it. "Sometimes school can be a nice distraction from

When Irina Slutskaya beat Michelle at Skate Canada in 1999, she knew it was time to adjust her school schedule.

Sasha Cohen, one of many young skaters now challenging Michelle

skating, breaking up the day," Michelle says. "Sometimes skating can be a good distraction from school. It's a lot. It's hard to play the catch-up game all the time."

Michelle adjusted her course schedule for the spring semester so she could devote more time to skating. But once again, she lost to Slutskaya—this time in the first big event of 2000, the Grand Prix Final. Michelle knew she had not yet found the right balance between school and skating, especially when a sore back bothered her at the U.S. Nationals a few weeks later. It didn't seem fair, but the reality was that Michelle had to work *harder* on her sport at a time when deep down she had really hoped to work *less*.

New challengers to Michelle now seemed to be coming out of the woodwork. In addition to Slutskaya, American Sasha Cohen was developing quickly into an elite-level skater. Soon she would be pushing Michelle, too. Coach Carroll tried to motivate

Once a crowd favorite because of her boundless energy and little-girl looks,
Michelle has become a mature and elegant world champion.

Michelle through the media. Whenever he was interviewed, he made sure to say things that would get Michelle fired up. "The gauntlet has definitely been thrown down," he told one reporter. "If she wants to pick it up, she has to schedule her time better."

Michelle knew her coach was right. Yet she also felt that her years of experience counted for something in competition. At the Nationals, she proved this after Cohen electrified the audience with an amazing series of combinations. Michelle took the ice and won over the judges with her supreme style. Though Cohen was flashier and more exciting, Michelle was now the total package. When she finished her long program, she had her fourth U.S. title. This one was especially gratifying—it was not an easy win. "I'm proud of myself," Michelle says. "I was strong...I didn't give an inch."

Put Up or Shut Up

"A lot of people think I'm going to turn pro…that's not where I want to be right now."
MICHELLE KWAN

Incredible as it sounds, some people in skating were saying that Michelle would soon be "over the hill"—too old to stay on top of her sport. They pointed to the fact that all of her past challengers had quit the amateur ranks and turned pro. They now worked for ice shows, skating night after night, traveling from city to city. Although this can be a challenging and rewarding career, these skaters are no longer interested in pushing the limits of their sport. Their main focus is entertainment. Most people expected Michelle to turn pro, too. She certainly would have made millions on tour.

Michelle kept saying that she had no interest. After her win at the 2000 Nationals, she confirmed the fact that she would remain focused on the 2002 Olympics. "I might not be professional ever," she said. "You might see me until 2006. This is what I love

Michelle soaks up the applause after finishing a routine at the 2000 World Championships. Moments like this make it hard for her to imagine ever turning pro.

"I think she's learned more and more that you can't hold back and achieve anything."

FRANK CARROLL

doing. You might not see a smiling, happy face all the time, but this is where I want to be. Deep down I feel it."

Michelle definitely felt it in April at the World Championships in France. In third place going into the long program, Michelle demonstrated her unflinching poise as she executed a difficult mix of jumps. Skating to a somber piece from the soundtrack of *The Red Violin*, she flowed throughout her routine, landing the only successful triple-toe/triple-toe combination of the entire competition. When leaders Irina Slutskaya and Mariya Butyrskaya could not match her, Michelle skated off with her third world title. It was quite a performance. "I think this was the most satisfying championship for me," she says. "There was a lot of pressure from outside: 'You've got to do triple-triple; got to do this; got to up the ante.' My dad always laughs at me and says I have to be up against the wall to fight back."

14-year-old Sarah Hughes, who gave Michelle a scare at the 2001 U.S. Nationals.

In October of 2000, Michelle got a reminder of how tough it is to stay on top of her sport. At Skate America, she did not hit a triple-loop cleanly and nearly lost to yet another kid, 14-year-old Sarah Hughes. Although she captured this event for the fifth time, Michelle was back under the microscope again. The whispers began later in the month at Skate Canada, when she finished second to Slutskaya.

Michelle's three-year plan entered its final phase in 2001. Her original goal was to maintain her competitive edge and nail down a spot on the 2002 Olympic team. Now there was more at stake. She wanted to shut up her critics once and for all. She wanted to win the U.S. Nationals *and* the World Championships.

As the Nationals approached, Michelle pulled herself together. She knew she would have to be extra-focused, but also stay relaxed. And she would have to ignore the fact that the judging to which she would be

Did You Know?

With her win in France, Michelle became the first woman to win three World Championships—and the first to twice reclaim her crown after losing it the year before.

Did You Know?

In 2001, Michelle joined Tenley Albright (above), Janet Lynn, and Peggy Fleming as the only skaters to win five U.S. championships.

subjected might not be entirely fair. In many ways, Michelle had become a victim of her own excellence—in order to continue receiving high marks, she had to be better each time out.

If that is how it had to be, then that is how it *would* be. Michelle arrived in Boston hungrier than ever. In her short program, she offered her most inspired performance in years, earning seven perfect marks. The press wanted to know what was "different." Michelle gave credit to Lori Nichol, who had retooled her routine and added more upbeat music. Privately, Michelle recognized that it had been a special night—the kind of night that you remember your entire life. "Just being out there and being in the moment, that's what all skaters dream of, feeling that sweet spot," she says. "That's what I felt."

Michelle's Achievements

1992
  1st Place, Southwest Pacific Regionals (Junior)

1993
  1st Place, Olympic Festival (Junior)

1994
  Gold Medalist, World Junior Championships
  Member, U.S. Olympic Team

1995
  1st Place, Skate America

1996
  Gold Medalist, World Championships
  Gold medalist, U.S. Nationals
  1st Place, Skate America

1997
  1st Place, Skate America

1998
  Gold Medalist, World Championships
  Gold Medalist, U.S. Nationals
  Gold Medalist, Goodwill Games
  Silver Medalist, Olympic Games
  Member U.S. Olympic Team

1999
  Gold medalist, U.S. Nationals
  1st Place, Skate America

2000
  Gold Medalist, World Championships
  Gold Medalist, U.S. Nationals
  1st Place, Skate America

2001
  Gold Medalist, World Championships
  Gold Medalist, U.S. Nationals

2002
  Member, U.S. Olympic Team

Michelle's Awards

Dial Award for top Scholar-Athlete 1997, 1998
Women's Sports Foundation Sportswoman of the Year 1998
U.S. Olympic Committee Athlete of the Year 1996, 1998, 1999
SKATING MAGAZINE Skater of the Year 1994, 1996, 1998
Chevrolet Perfect 6 Award 1998

World Beater

CHAPTER 9

*"She tugs at
your heartstrings.
Few skaters can do that."*
FRANK CARROLL

A few weeks after Michelle's victory in Boston, the top international competitors gathered in Japan for the Grand Prix Final. Michelle lost to Irina Slutskaya, who nailed a dazzling triple-lutz/double-loop combination. This sent the Kwan team back to the drawing board. Based on this defeat, Coach Carroll and Michelle agreed that to win at the upcoming Worlds, she would have to pull off a perfect triple-triple combination.

After some intense practices, Michelle was totally locked-in for the World Championships. And it showed. Her blades barely seemed to break the ice at times, and her jumps were sensational. She hit her combinations just right, including a triple-toe/triple-toe, and won her fourth world championship. "I was gutsy," Michelle said afterwards. "I did everything I planned. No backing up, adding things, subtracting things. I just let myself go."

Michelle and Frank Carroll watch with pride as she receives seven perfect 6's at the 2001 U.S. Nationals. In October 2001—just a few months before the Winter Olympics—Michelle ended her long partnership with Carroll, surprising many in the skating world.

Irina Slutskaya (left) and Sarah Hughes (right) join Michelle on the
victory stand at the 2001 U.S. Nationals.

After winning four world titles and five national ones, Michelle has to be considered among the finest skaters in history. In a sport where careers burn and flicker like birthday candles, she has been a beacon of consistency and excellence. No one in the modern era has skated so well for so long. The 2002 season will mark her eighth year at or near the top of her sport. In that time she has become a sister to some, a daughter to others, and a role model of the highest magnitude. If Michelle should add Olympic gold to her trophy case, she would have to be considered the greatest athlete ever to lace up a pair of figure skates.

With her spot on the U.S. Olympic team all but assured, everyone wanted to know what Michelle planned to do *after* the 2002 Winter Games. She shocked the skating world with her reply. The ultimate competitor, Michelle said that not only would she consider skating in the 2006 Olympics—she was not ruling out 2010!

"I'm serious," she smiles. "If I have that desire, if I want to be the best, if I want to keep on competing and still have that flame burning, then why not?"

Michelle sports a different look on the cover of SPORTS ILLUSTRATED FOR WOMEN. Relaxed and confident, she is learning to enjoy life at the top.

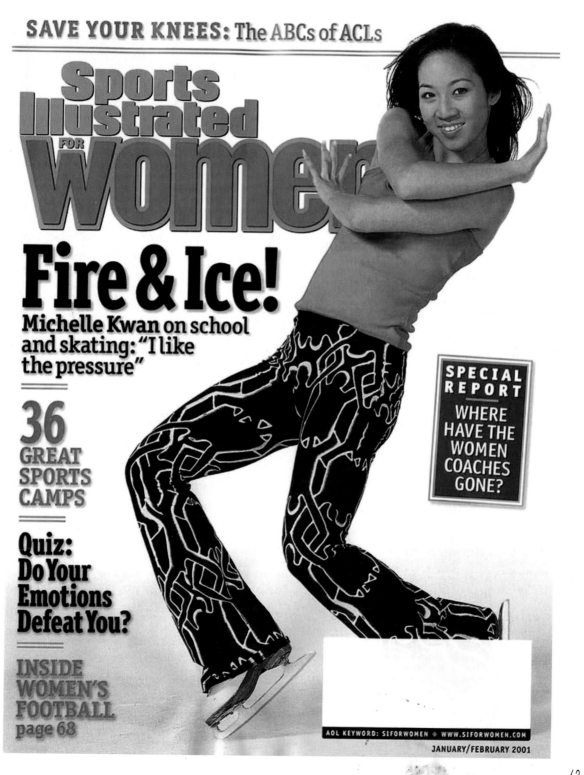

SAVE YOUR KNEES: The ABCs of ACLs

Sports Illustrated FOR Women

Fire & Ice!

Michelle Kwan on school and skating: "I like the pressure"

36 GREAT SPORTS CAMPS

Quiz: Do Your Emotions Defeat You?

INSIDE WOMEN'S FOOTBALL page 68

SPECIAL REPORT

WHERE HAVE THE WOMEN COACHES GONE?

AOL KEYWORD: SIFORWOMEN ✦ WWW.SIFORWOMEN.COM

JANUARY/FEBRUARY 2001

63

Index